WebSocket Essentials – Building Apps with HTML5 WebSockets

Build your own real-time web applications using HTML5 WebSockets

Varun Chopra

open source
community experience distilled

PUBLISHING

BIRMINGHAM - MUMBAI

WebSocket Essentials – Building Apps with HTML5 WebSockets

Copyright © 2015 Packt Publishing

First published: April 2015

Production reference: 1270415

Published by Packt Publishing Ltd.
Livery Place
35 Livery Street
Birmingham B3 2PB, UK.

ISBN 978-1-78439-675-6

www.packtpub.com

Credits

Author
Varun Chopra

Reviewers
Adir Amsalem
Sann-Remy Chea

Commissioning Editor
Amarabha Banerjee

Acquisition Editor
Sonali Vernekar

Content Development Editor
Mamata Walkar

Technical Editor
Siddhesh Patil

Copy Editors
Puja Lalwani
Vikrant Phadke

Project Coordinator
Shipra Chawhan

Proofreaders
Safis Editing
Paul Hindle

Indexer
Monica Mehta

Production Coordinator
Aparna Bhagat

Cover Work
Aparna Bhagat

About the Author

Varun Chopra has a lot of experience in the design and development of enterprise applications. He has worked as a consultant and has extensive experience in integrating different technologies. Besides his love of technology, he is also a singer and a guitarist and loves gadgets.

About the Reviewers

Adir Amsalem is a software engineer from Israel. Since the age of 16, he has loved developing websites and web apps, reading about technology, and solving technological challenges. He currently works for a major financial institution, where he leads web and frontend development of several products. Previously, he was a web developer and frontend developer at several Israeli companies and was also a freelancer.

Sann-Remy Chea works as a software engineer at Ubisoft Owlient, a video game company specializing in web and mobile games, based in Paris, France. He has also worked at IBM as an application architect intern. Fond of web application development, he specializes in JavaScript and Node.js.

www.PacktPub.com

Support files, eBooks, discount offers, and more

For support files and downloads related to your book, please visit www.PacktPub.com.

Did you know that Packt offers eBook versions of every book published, with PDF and ePub files available? You can upgrade to the eBook version at www.PacktPub.com and as a print book customer, you are entitled to a discount on the eBook copy. Get in touch with us at service@packtpub.com for more details.

At www.PacktPub.com, you can also read a collection of free technical articles, sign up for a range of free newsletters and receive exclusive discounts and offers on Packt books and eBooks.

https://www2.packtpub.com/books/subscription/packtlib

Do you need instant solutions to your IT questions? PacktLib is Packt's online digital book library. Here, you can search, access, and read Packt's entire library of books.

Why subscribe?

- Fully searchable across every book published by Packt
- Copy and paste, print, and bookmark content
- On demand and accessible via a web browser

Free access for Packt account holders

If you have an account with Packt at www.PacktPub.com, you can use this to access PacktLib today and view 9 entirely free books. Simply use your login credentials for immediate access.

Table of Contents

Preface

HTML, the most important part of web development, was lacking somewhere, but now developers are returning to HTML5 because of its enhancements and features, giving them a new experience of development. WebSocket support on different browsers made it easier to develop web applications with a lot of features.

Data communication between the client and the server is one of the most important parts of any web application. Almost all browsers support WebSockets, which makes it more powerful and available. Developers always want to build their application on a concrete ground so that it is reliable for users. WebSocket makes this possible now. With HTML5 enhancements, it is being accepted and appreciated widely in the community.

In this book, you will learn and understand how WebSockets with HTML5 can create great applications, especially applications where data needs to be pushed from both the client side and the server side. With some basic sample applications that we will create in this book, you will understand how the client can be set up and how the Node.js-based WebSocket server can be created with ease.

This book is for developers who want to learn to create WebSocket-based applications. It gives you real-world scenarios for implementing different aspects of communication with WebSockets. It is simple to learn and easy to understand.

What this book covers

Chapter 1, Introducing the World of Web App, is an introduction to web applications, covering the basics of the Web. This chapter introduces HTML5, its new features and WebSockets.

Chapter 2, Getting Started with WebSockets, covers WebSockets in depth, including the benefits of WebSockets and how to create a sample application. Here, you learn to create your own basic WebSocket server using the Node.js platform.

Chapter 3, Configuring the Server and Transferring Real–time Data, shows how data can be sent across different users connected to the server using WebSockets. This chapter also covers the creation of an application using the JavaScript library to share a presentation and collaboratively change slides between different users.

Chapter 4, Using WebSockets in Real Scenario, demonstrates another application to explain more about how WebSockets can be used in real-world scenarios. This chapter also talks about the JavaScript framework and its uses.

Chapter 5, WebSockets for Mobile and Tablet, covers how WebSockets behaves with mobile devices, different libraries for mobile WebSockets, running the server on an Android mobile phone, and the use of the Express.js package for delivering content from within the server.

Chapter 6, Enhancing HTML5 Web Application Development Using Modern Tools, explains different tools and techniques that can be used to enhance web application development. This chapter illustrates speeding up development using different tools such as editors, package mangers, version control, boilerplates, application frameworks, responsive web design, and more.

What you need for this book

You will need a machine that has a modern browser installed on it, primarily a browser that supports WebSockets and HTML5. You'll also require a text editor, such as Sublime Text. Further, it is necessary to install Node.js if you don't have it.

To check whether your browser supports WebSockets and HTML5 or not, go to `http://www.caniuse.com`.

Who this book is for

This book is for web developers with a basic knowledge of HTML and JavaScript. It focuses on implementing different applications and gives hands-on experience to developers. It is a fast book and it equips you with the necessary tools and techniques for developing WebSocket-based applications.

Conventions

In this book, you will find a number of text styles that distinguish between different kinds of information. Here are some examples of these styles and an explanation of their meaning.

Code words in text, database table names, folder names, filenames, file extensions, pathnames, dummy URLs, user input, and Twitter handles are shown as follows: "Here, Host is the name of the server that we are hitting."

A block of code is set as follows:

```html
<html>

<head>
<meta charset="utf-8" >
<title>WebSocket Test</title>
<script language="javascript" type="text/javascript">
var wsUri = "ws://echo.websocket.org/";
var output;
```

New terms and **important words** are shown in bold. Words that you see on the screen, for example, in menus or dialog boxes, appear in the text like this: "Take a look at the **Console** log in the left-hand-side window."

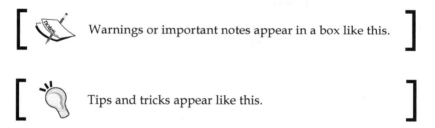

Warnings or important notes appear in a box like this.

Tips and tricks appear like this.

Reader feedback

Feedback from our readers is always welcome. Let us know what you think about this book — what you liked or disliked. Reader feedback is important for us as it helps us develop titles that you will really get the most out of.

To send us general feedback, simply e-mail feedback@packtpub.com, and mention the book's title in the subject of your message.

If there is a topic that you have expertise in and you are interested in either writing or contributing to a book, see our author guide at www.packtpub.com/authors.

Customer support

Now that you are the proud owner of a Packt book, we have a number of things to help you to get the most from your purchase.

Downloading the example code

You can download the example code files from your account at `http://www.packtpub.com` for all the Packt Publishing books you have purchased. If you purchased this book elsewhere, you can visit `http://www.packtpub.com/support` and register to have the files e-mailed directly to you.

Errata

Although we have taken every care to ensure the accuracy of our content, mistakes do happen. If you find a mistake in one of our books—maybe a mistake in the text or the code—we would be grateful if you could report this to us. By doing so, you can save other readers from frustration and help us improve subsequent versions of this book. If you find any errata, please report them by visiting `http://www.packtpub.com/submit-errata`, selecting your book, clicking on the **Errata Submission Form** link, and entering the details of your errata. Once your errata are verified, your submission will be accepted and the errata will be uploaded to our website or added to any list of existing errata under the Errata section of that title.

To view the previously submitted errata, go to `https://www.packtpub.com/books/content/support` and enter the name of the book in the search field. The required information will appear under the **Errata** section.

Piracy

Piracy of copyrighted material on the Internet is an ongoing problem across all media. At Packt, we take the protection of our copyright and licenses very seriously. If you come across any illegal copies of our works in any form on the Internet, please provide us with the location address or website name immediately so that we can pursue a remedy.

Please contact us at `copyright@packtpub.com` with a link to the suspected pirated material.

We appreciate your help in protecting our authors and our ability to bring you valuable content.

Questions

If you have a problem with any aspect of this book, you can contact us at `questions@packtpub.com`, and we will do our best to address the problem.

1

Introducing the World of Web App

Web application development has reached the next level with HTML5 and WebSockets. The revolutionary enhancements in web development technologies have equipped developers with modern tools and techniques. Using WebSockets they can create web applications which can send data not only from the client side but from the server side as well. Web applications with real-time data transfer can be created with a lot lower use of bandwidth. WebSockets by complementing HTML5 enhanced feature can make future applications powerful. Let's talk about the basics of the Web before understanding WebSockets in detail.

What is the Web?

The foundation of the Web was laid in the late eighties. The Web works on interlinked hypertext documents that we can access using the Internet. A browser plays a vital role in reading and converting these hypertext documents into a readable and more meaningful format, which we call web pages. HTML5 is the hypertext document which the browser reads and renders for us. The browser not only reads and renders but also creates a **Document Object Model (DOM)** for us so that we can read and manipulate the structure easily. Dynamic manipulation of the DOM can be achieved by the JavaScript language, which is a standard scripting language for HTML. A server plays a vital role in the functioning of the Web. We mainly consider the Web to be divided into two parts: client and server. Client is considered to be the browser whereas server is the one who gives client the data.

Let's see how the Web works:

1. Browser requests a URL from server.
2. Server checks and returns the HTML file.
3. Browser engine draws the page.

In a nutshell, this is how the Web works. Browsers and servers are the most important entities of the Web. Browsers have engines that read HTML files and render web applications in the way HTML files are described. Different browsers such as Blink, Trident, Gecko, WebKit, and so on, have different engines to render the HTML of a page. Now servers are the one who are storing all the data and providing the same on user request.

Web applications

In the beginning of the Web, pages were static. They only used to show content with minimal interactivity and functionality. But with the advancement in the standards of the Web along with the evolution of computers, efficient browsers, enhanced tools and libraries, creating web applications has now become very easy, and a lot of functionalities can be added very quickly.

Here is a simple definition of web applications—any application that runs on a browser is a web application. There are many web applications that we use in our daily routine to check mails, read news, watch videos, and so on. Web applications run in your browser and do not require much of your computer resources.

The Web is growing at a very high rate. Many companies are building their applications on the Web. The first and most important benefit is that it is independent of the operating system. You can run it on Windows, Mac, or Linux and it works the same, because the work is mainly done by the browsers and they are available for most operating systems.

Here are some of the examples of web applications:

*   Gmail
*   Dropbox
*   Flickr
*   Facebook

Where does WebSockets fit?

As we have seen some examples of web applications, now the question here is where does WebSockets fit in these applications or any web application? Let us first understand something about application behavior; let us take an example of **Gmail**, which is basically a mailing client. The work of a mailing client is to fetch mails and display them. This sounds simple, but the problem arises when someone sends you a mail and you want that mail to be displayed right away. To implement such a functionality there are different ways, such as polling and long-polling, which are not efficient. So WebSockets solves the problem here by providing a server push facility. WebSockets provides functionality to push from both the client and server side, which makes it stand out.

WebSockets comes with some good features and great benefits over other methods of communication. Some of the features and benefits of WebSockets are:

- Full-duplex communication
- Low bandwidth consumption
- Security
- Low latency
- Works over **Transmission Control Protocol** (**TCP**) (although it needs HTTP for initial handshake)
- Supported by almost all the web browsers and web servers including mobile browsers

We can treat WebSockets as a feature which enhances the experience of web applications. And with HTML5-enhanced features, we can create a dynamic and real-time application.

WebSockets over other methods

There are different ways of implementing data communication between a client and server. **Flash**, **Comet**, **PusherApp**, and so on provide us with the features needed to implement the data communication which WebSockets provides. Then the question arises that why should we go with WebSockets? There are many reasons for picking WebSockets over other methods, some of which are as follows:

- In comparison to other means of data communication, WebSockets exhibits low latency, which decreases from nearly 150 ms to 50 ms.
- WebSockets is a lightweight connection and uses low bandwidth.

- It requires lesser developer effort in terms of learning and implementation in different technologies.
- Ease of compilation when different technologies are used.
- Code maintenance becomes easy with WebSockets.
- WebSockets offers full-duplex connection support without much overhead.

Modern browsers

Modern browsers are equipped with advanced features to support web applications.

Web applications have a lot of different features, and to support those features, we need browsers—not just ordinary but modern browsers. For a modern browser to support the advanced features provided by HTML5, it has to implement the HTML5 standard, because it has the latest features and functionalities. There are some versions of browsers that do not support HTML5 majorly because they have not implemented the HTML5 standards, either because they were developed earlier or they choose not to.

Some of the advantages of modern browsers are as follows:

- Good performance
- Good security
- Lesser issues
- Faster page loading
- Experimental **Application Programming Interface** or **API**
- Support for latest features
- Access to native resources

HTML

HTML is a markup language which is used by browsers to render a webpage. It is the standard fixed by the **World Wide Web (W3)**. This standard has some defined elements which different browsers implements.

HTML5 – the modern Web standard

After eight years working on the HTML5 standard, W3 finalized the standard on October 28, 2014. This standard is going to be revolutionary for the future of the Web. The enhancements done to the HTML standard are revolutionary. Let us go through the main features of HTML5, which makes it a great standard for the Web:

Media – audio/video

One of the big features introduced in the HTML5 standard is media playback. We can now play audio/video directly using the browser. Earlier we used to use some plugins in order to play audio and video, which added another layer onto our web application. For example, **YouTube** used Flash player to play videos, but now we can play the videos directly. This feature has been a bigger advantage for applications which are completely built using HTML.

Along with playback of audio and video, we can also capture audio and video resources of the device. Accessing the camera and microphone can be done using the getUserMedia() API, but it is still not available to all browsers because it is an experimental feature; it is, however, a feature that is greatly needed. This API not only gives access to the desktop computer, but also to the camera and microphone in mobile and tablet devices. This is another feature which will remove the dependency on different plugins for media access and capturing.

Canvas

Canvas gives you per pixel access for manipulation at runtime. So you can draw shapes, render graphs, color them, manipulate them, and even manipulate bitmap images per pixel, along with many more features. The canvas feature gives us an upper hand in drawing and making web applications just like Microsoft Paint (formerly Microsoft Paintbrush) or Adobe Photoshop.

The canvas element has a different set of methods to create drawings using lines, circles, boxes, text, graphics, and so on. JavaScript is used to draw in the canvas container.

Form elements

There are many enhancements in form elements which help us create a great experience for the users and are easy to manage from the developers' perspective. Validation was a big problem earlier; we had to write our own code for it, but now it is a part of the elements. There are some enhancements which are made keeping mobile devices in mind, such as field type keyboard—for example, a dedicated keyboard for numeric fields. Some of the new elements are:

- **Input**: The following are the input types:
    - `type="email"`: A field with inbuilt email validator
    - `type="url"`: A field with inbuilt URL validator
    - `type="number"`: A field with inbuilt number input restriction and validator
    - `type="range"`: A range slider with max and min function
- **Datalist**: It specifies a predefined list of options for list control.
- **Keygen**: This element provides secure data submission using the public/private key method. From the security point of view, it is an excellent enhancement.
- **Output**: This element helps in showing the output value during form filling.

Semantics

Semantics are elements which have a meaning. Every developer wants to code in a language that is easy to understand and implement. Semantics is what makes it easier to read and understand the code because it defines the meaning of that piece of element or tag. Some examples of semantic elements are `<audio>`, `<video>`, `<form>`, and `<table>`. Examples of non-semantic elements include `<div>` and `<span>`. We can see from the examples that non-semantic elements don't tell us about the content, while semantic elements tell us clearly about the content.

Some of the new semantics in HTML5 are as follows:

- `<section>`
- `<nav>`
- `<article>`
- `<aside>`
- `<hgroup>`
- `<header>`
- `<footer>`

The addition of these new elements will help in making the code more readable and meaningful. And now let me introduce you to custom elements. Yes, now we can make our own custom elements using JavaScript, either by creating them from scratch or extending the default set of DOM elements by adding new behaviors to them. This way we can create different sets of reusable web components and use them across our web application. This feature adds meaning to the code and is a big advantage for large-scale applications to make reusable web components.

Mobile first

HTML5 and CSS3 standards are made keeping mobile devices in mind. There are many enhancements that optimize the code for mobile/tablet devices. Mobiles have evolved to an extent where they have become a part of our daily lives. We have started browsing the Internet more on mobile/tablet devices. And HTML5 has given a lot of power to the Web to match up to the modern Web requirements. HTML5 and CSS3 have some excellent features which can deliver the same content for all devices: desktop, mobile, and tablets. Some of the important features include the following:

- **Viewport**: This helps in adjusting the view of webpages based on devices. We can set a different scale level and so on.
- **Media queries**: CSS as per the screen size; isn't it a brilliant feature? Now by using media queries the CSS styling can be changed at runtime. Responsive web design is a very important feature of modern Web. We need the content to be displayed as per the screen size, and it should adapt and show appropriate content eliminating the not so important content from the page for smaller size devices.
- **Touch events**: These are vital events for mobile/tablet devices. **Swipe** is one of the important events that is now a part of HTML5 DOM.

Offline storage

The world is emerging with different technologies and we widely use online and web services in order to create an effective work space and a web world that will cater to our professional and personal needs. There are scenarios where you need websites to be accessible offline, that is, without an active internet connection on your device. This can be achieved using the offline storage functionality. Once you have opened a webpage, it is possible to put the data in cache so that next time you open it or for some reason your connection is lost, you can still open and use it.

The offline system is quite important when the data needs to be stored locally for the user. Mainly when it comes to reloading or restoring the pages if the system is in offline mode.

So, whenever we open a URL, it basically hits the server and then the server returns the requested file. Then, the browser renders the file which was given by the server. Now in case we are offline, the browser will take control, and instead of hitting the server to get the file, it loads the files from its local copy which was cached when we opened it earlier. There is also an API which tells us that we are online or offline. It is very helpful in case of mobile/tablet devices where the connectivity can be lost at any point of time.

Geolocation

There are many applications which use geolocation, such as Twitter, Facebook, Foursquare, Google Maps, and so on. The introduction of this feature as a part of HTML5 has made it easier for developers to get the location of their device.

Mobile and tablet devices have **Global Positioning System (GPS)**, and using this API, the hardware of the device can be accessed. Let's take an example of an application where you want to find nearby hotels. Using GPS, your location can be detected and a corresponding list of nearby hotels can be provided. This feature has reduced the effort of developers in implementing features related to geolocation. And yes, it is a feature which needs users' permission to work. A prompt is given to the user to allow the web application to access their location details.

Drag and drop

Drag and drop is a feature which was always there but could only be implemented using some plugins. The good news is that now it is a part of HTML5 standard. By leveraging this feature, a lot of new controls can be defined, as we also have the custom semantics feature which we can use to define our own custom controls.

Web applications use a lot of different controls or widgets to display the data in a more user-friendly way. For large-scale applications where lists and grids are the most important controls to display the data, drag and drop plays a very important role. Controls that show calendars or the timeline of a project need the drag-and-drop feature to make it more usable. Some of the basic interactions are:

- Rearranging items in a list
- Moving items from one list to another
- Rearranging layouts
- Dragging items around the canvas
- Dragging a file from the computer to the browser

There are many good examples of drag-and-drop features. Different companies have implemented and made their own component library, which implements the drag-and-drop feature. Some examples are Sencha, jQueryUI, KineticJS, Kendo UI, and so on.

Web workers

Web workers are just JavaScript running in background. JavaScript is mainly used to manipulate the HTML of a webpage at runtime and uses only one main thread. Web workers have made it possible to run a piece of JavaScript code in the background without affecting the current process. Normally, whenever we run a process in JavaScript, it runs in a queue fashion, which means that one process is executed at a time. It blocks the whole UI for some time and you can't click on buttons as well. This has had a huge impact on the application performance. That is one of the reasons why bigger web applications hesitate in choosing HTML, but web workers will surely change this.

JavaScript

HTML pages are static; to make them dynamic and interactive, JavaScript is used. JavaScript is called the language of the Web. It is based on **ECMAScript**, and every browser runs JavaScript. All the interactivity from the clicking of a button, navigation to pages, calling services, and so on is done by JavaScript.

There are many frameworks built using JavaScript to make scripting easier to use: one of the majorly used frameworks is jQuery. It gives a user the flexibility to use DOM events, features, and API in a readable and meaningful way.

Modern servers

JavaScript is improving at a quick rate. Most developers are now using JavaScript for client-side handling. Introduction of the **Node.js** server has changed the scope of work of developers. Earlier, developers used different servers, and for that, they had to learn lot of different languages. Node.js removed that gap and gave developers a platform where they could build a server which is JavaScript based.

JavaScript servers built on the Node.js platform are quite simple to use and increase productivity as well. Developers can make a server and run it in very less time. Creating a server in Node.js is very easy and has many features, such as real-time data transfer using different packages available. There are many frameworks which are built for Node.js, such as **Express.js**, which helps in speeding up the development process.

Node.js is free platform and provides a lot of different packages which can be distributed freely. The **Node Package Manager** (**NPM**) manages the dependencies for an application. It also is a version manager.

WebSockets

With the growth in web applications, the need for real-time data which supports full-duplex communication has also increased. Real-time communication is always hard to implement, and people used Flash for the same. The reason Flash-like plugins are used is because this feature was missing in HTML standard. So whenever we wanted to implement such mechanisms in HTML, we used the polling mechanism, which is a very costly process in terms of performance.

HTML5 comes prepared for all the required features needs for a good web application. WebSockets is a part of HTML5 standard and the WebSocket API is fully available to be utilized.

WebSockets gives a full-duplex communication between the client and server, which basically allows data transfer easily and on need basis, unlike the polling mechanism where we keep hitting the server on an interval to check for changes. WebSockets can send data from the server or client side — basically a connection bridge is opened which allows data transfer from both sides. WebSockets has eliminated the use of third-party plugins giving HTML developers the ability to implement it directly using the WebSockets API.

Summary

We have seen what the important elements of modern Web are in this chapter, and the enhanced features HTML5 standard has brought to us. We have been introduced to WebSockets, and in the next chapter, we will see the implementation of WebSockets from both the client and server side.

2
Getting Started with WebSockets

Client server communication is one of the most important parts of any web application. Data communication between the server and client has to be smooth and fast so that the user can have an excellent experience. If we look into the traditional methods of server communication, we will find that those methods were limited and were not really the best solutions. These methods have been used by people for a long period of time and made HTML the second choice for data communication.

Why WebSockets?

The answer to why we need WebSockets lies in the question—what are the problems with the other methods of communication? Some of the methods used for server communication are request/response, polling, and long-polling, which have been explained as follows:

- Request/Response: This is a commonly used mechanisms in which the client requests the server and gets a response. This process is driven by some interaction like the click of a button on the webpage to refresh the whole page. When AJAX came into the picture, it made the webpages dynamic and helped in loading some part of the webpage without loading the whole page.

- Polling: There are scenarios where we need the data to be reflected without user interaction, such as the score of a football match. In polling, the data is fetched after a period of time and it keeps hitting the server, regardless of whether the data has changed or not. This causes unnecessary calls to the server, opening a connection and then closing it every time.

- Long-polling: This is basically a connection kept open for a particular time period. This is one of the ways of achieving real-time communication, but it works only when you know the time interval.

The problems with these methods lead to the solution, which is WebSockets. It solves all the problems faced during the use of the old methods.

Importance of WebSockets

WebSockets comes into the picture to save us from the old heavy methods of server communication. WebSockets solved one of the biggest problems of server communication by providing a full-duplex two-way communication bridge. It provides both the server and client the ability to send data at any point of time, which was not provided by any of the old methods. This has not only improved performance but also reduced the latency of data. It creates a lightweight connection which we can keep open for a long time without sacrificing the performance. It also gives us full control to open and close the connection at any point of time.

WebSockets comes as a part of HTML5 standard, so we do not need to worry about adding some extra plugin to make it work. WebSockets API is fully supported and implemented by JavaScript. Almost all modern browsers now support WebSockets; this can be checked using the website `http://caniuse.com/#feat=websockets` which gives the following screenshot:

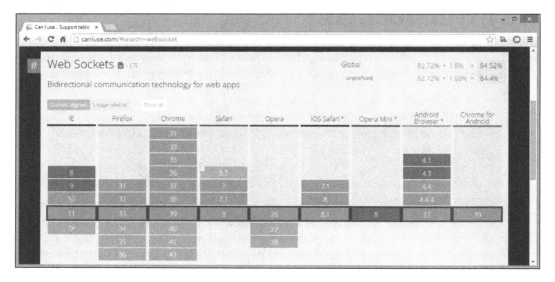

WebSockets need to be implemented on both the client and server side. On the client side, the API is a part of HTML5. But on the server side, we need to use a library that implements WebSockets. There are many—or we can say almost all—servers that support WebSockets API libraries now. Node.js, which is a modern JavaScript based platform also supports WebSockets based server implementation using different packages, which makes it really easy for developers to code both server and client-side code without learning another language.

When to use?

WebSockets being a very powerful way of communication between the client and server, it is really useful for applications which need a lot of server interaction. As WebSockets gives us the benefit of real-time communication, applications that require real-time data transfer, like chatting applications, can leverage WebSockets. It is not only used for real-time communication but also for scenarios where we need only the server to push the data to the client.

The decision to use WebSockets can be made when we know the exact purpose of its usage. We should not use WebSockets when we just have to create a website with static pages and hardly any interaction. We should use WebSockets where the communication is higher in terms of data passing between the client and server.

There are many applications like stock applications where the data keeps updating in real time. Collaborative applications need real-time data sharing, such as a game of chess or a Ping-Pong game. WebSockets is majorly utilized in real-time gaming web applications.

How it works?

WebSockets communicates using the TCP layer. The connection is established over HTTP and is basically a handshake mechanism between the client and server. After the handshake, the connection is upgraded to TCP. Let's see how it works through this flow diagram:

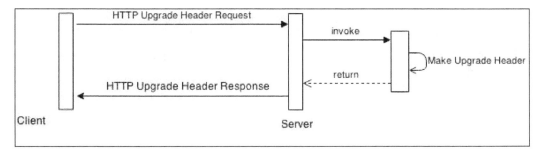

The following steps will take you through the flow shown in the preceding diagram:

1. The first step is the HTTP call that is initiated from the client side; the header of the HTTP call looks like this:

```
GET /chat HTTP/1.1
Host: server.example.com
Upgrade: websocket
Connection: Upgrade
Sec-WebSocket-Key: x3JJHMbDL1EzLkh9GBhXDw==
Sec-WebSocket-Protocol: chat, superchat
Sec-WebSocket-Version: 13
Origin: http://example.com
```

   ° Here, Host is the name of the server that we are hitting.

   ° Upgrade shows that it is an upgrade call for, in this case, WebSockets. Connection defines that it is an upgrade call.

   ° Sec-Websocket-Key is a randomly generated key which is further used to authenticate the response. It is the authentication key of the handshake.

   ° Origin is also another important parameter which shows where the call originated from; on the server side, it is used to check the requester's authenticity.

2. Once the server checks the authenticity a response is sent back, which looks like this:

```
HTTP/1.1 101 Switching Protocols
Upgrade: websocket
Connection: Upgrade
Sec-WebSocket-Accept: HSmrc0sMlYUkAGmm5OPpG2HaGWk=
Sec-WebSocket-Protocol: chat
```

   ° Here, Sec-WebSocket-Accept has a key which is decoded and checked with the key sent for confirmation that the response is coming to the right originator.

3. So, once the connection is open, the client and server can send the data to each other.

4. The data is sent in the form of small packets using TCP protocol. These calls are not HTTP so they are not visible directly under the Network tab of Developer Tools of a browser.

WebSocket API

WebSockets standard is defined by W3. The API interface for WebSockets looks like this:

```
enum BinaryType { "blob", "arraybuffer" };

[Constructor(DOMString url, optional (DOMString or DOMString[])
protocols), Exposed=Window,Worker]

interface WebSocket : EventTarget {

  readonly attribute DOMString url;

  // ready state

  const unsigned short CONNECTING = 0;
  const unsigned short OPEN = 1;
  const unsigned short CLOSING = 2;
  const unsigned short CLOSED = 3;
  readonly attribute unsigned short readyState;
  readonly attribute unsigned long bufferedAmount;

  // networking

          attribute EventHandler onopen;
          attribute EventHandler onerror;
          attribute EventHandler onclose;
  readonly attribute DOMString extensions;
  readonly attribute DOMString protocol;

  void close([Clamp] optional unsigned short code, optional
DOMString reason);

  // messaging
          attribute EventHandler onmessage;
          attribute BinaryType binaryType;
  void send(DOMString data);
  void send(Blob data);
  void send(ArrayBuffer data);
  void send(ArrayBufferView data);

};
```

We can see from the interface the types of ready states, networking events, and types of messages that WebSockets API provides.

> **Downloading the example code**
>
> You can download the example code files from your account at http://www.packtpub.com for all the Packt Publishing books you have purchased. If you purchased this book elsewhere, you can visit http://www.packtpub.com/support and register to have the files e-mailed directly to you.

Ready states

Following are the ready states:

- **CONNECTING**: The connection has not yet been established.
- **OPEN**: The WebSockets connection is established and communication is possible.
- **CLOSING**: The connection is going through the closing handshake or the close() method has been invoked.
- **CLOSED**: The connection has been closed or could not be opened.

Events

Following are the events triggered:

- **onopen**: Triggered when the connection is opened.
- **onclose**: Triggered when the connection is closed.
- **onerror**: Triggered when an error is encountered.
- **onmessage**: Triggered when a message is received from the server.

Echo Test

Let us start with the **Echo Test** application. Go to the URL https://www.websocket.org/echo.html. Here you can see a readymade **Echo** server which we can hit and then receive a message. It just gives you a server; when you send a message to this server it will send the same message in return. Go ahead and play with your Echo application. After this, we will see how to write our own client code to hit this Echo server.

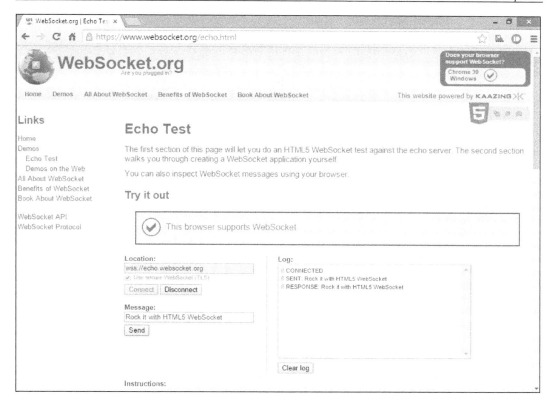

The WebSockets client app

Let us start with writing client-side code in JavaScript. We will be hitting the same Echo server for now. Let's get started with our client-side code. Here is how the client code will look:

```html
<!DOCTYPE html>
<html>
  <head>
    <meta charset="utf-8" >
    <title>WebSocket Test</title>
    <script language="javascript" type="text/javascript">
      var wsUri = "ws://echo.websocket.org/";
      var output;

      function init(){
          output = document.getElementById("output");
          testWebSocket();
      }
```

```
function testWebSocket(){

    websocket = new WebSocket(wsUri);

    websocket.onopen = onOpen;

    websocket.onclose = onClose;

    websocket.onmessage = onMessage;

    websocket.onerror = onError;

}

function onOpen(evt){
    writeToScreen("CONNECTED");
    doSend("WebSocket rocks");
}

function onClose(evt){
    writeToScreen("DISCONNECTED");
}

function onMessage(evt){
    writeToScreen('<span style="color: blue;">RESPONSE: ' +
evt.data + '</span>');
    websocket.close();
}

function onError(evt){
    writeToScreen('<span style="color: red;">ERROR:</span> '
+ evt.data);
}

function doSend(message){
    writeToScreen("SENT: " + message);
    websocket.send(message);
}

function writeToScreen(message){
    var pre = document.createElement("p");
    pre.style.wordWrap = "break-word";
    pre.innerHTML = message;
    output.appendChild(pre);
}
```

```
        window.addEventListener("load", init, false);

    </script>
  </head>
  <body>
    <h2>WebSocket Test</h2>
    <div id="output"></div>
  </body>
</html>
```

If we run this code, we will get this output:

This is a pretty straightforward code; developers with a little experience in JavaScript can also understand it. Let's go through the code and understand what is happening. The sequence here is as follows:

1. We open the connection with the server.
2. If it is successful, then we send the message to the server.
3. Once we receive the message from the server, we display it.
4. Then, we close the connection.

Let's talk about the important phases that we need to take care of whenever we are going to create any application using WebSockets.

Instantiation

We can create an instance of a WebSockets object just like we create the instance of any other class. Here is how we can do it:

```
var wsUri = "ws://echo.websocket.org/";
websocket = new WebSocket(wsUri);
```

There is only one important parameter that we need to pass, and that is the URI of the server. You will notice that we have used the **ws://** URL schema, which basically defines which protocol should be used for the communication. There is another URL schema, that is, **wss://**, which is used in case we want to use the secure communication, just like we have HTTPS for a secure connection.

Adding events

We can add event handlers to a WebSockets object that are triggered in case of any event. There are four main events which we need to add handlers to and these are:

- When we create an instance of the WebSockets object, we get the open event triggered, which tells us that the connection is now open. Here is how we have added the event:

  ```
  websocket.onopen = onOpen;
  ```

- When the connection is closed, the `onClose` method is called:

  ```
  websocket.onclose = onClose;
  ```

- When we receive a message from a server, the `onmessage` event is triggered and we can handle it and get the data from it using the data property of the event:

  ```
  websocket.onmessage = onMessage;
  ```

- Sometimes we face some errors during connection because the server is down or some configuration issue has occurred, or due to other reasons. Due to these different possible reasons, we can get an error which is captured and given to the client in the `onerror` event handler:

  ```
  websocket.onerror = onError;
  ```

Sending messages

We can send not only strings but also objects, blobs, and array buffers as well to the server and vice versa. The send method is as follows:

```
websocket.send(message);
```

It is one of the important methods because we use it to send data to the server.

Receiving messages

Receiving data is also simple as we have already placed a handler for the event. So here we will get the data under the data property of the event object. In this scenario, we have added some styling and added that to the HTML page so that we can just have a visually attractive message, which we can see from the output:

```
function onMessage(evt){
    writeToScreen('<span style="color: blue;">RESPONSE: ' +
evt.data + '</span>');
}
```

Closing the connection

Connections also need to be closed; the best practice is to close the connection when we are done using it. Similarly we want the connection to the server to be closed once we receive the message. We have to make sure that we close the connection before exiting the application. We just simply have to call the close() method of the WebSocket object to close the open connection.The method to close the connection is as follows:

```
websocket.close();
```

The WebSocket server

We have seen how the client works and how we can send the data to the server and receive it from server. Now we will see how we can make our own server code handle the messages.

Using modern web technology, we will explore the implementation of the WebSocket server using Node.js. Node.js is a very friendly, lightweight, and easy-to-use platform. So let's see how we can make our own WebSockets server.

The Node.js server

The Node.js server gives us a lot of flexibility to create our own server. There are many library packages available via NPM. We will be using a library created by Einar Otto Stangvik which basically handles general mechanisms, such as upgrading the HTTP protocol and others. It is a very robust, clean, and lightweight library.

Now, to set up the server you must have Node.js installed on your machine. If you don't have it installed, then go ahead and check out the website of Node. js (https://nodejs.org/), read the documentation, and install it. Refer to the following steps to install WebSocket server:

1. Create a new project in Node.js using NPM. You just need to run the npm init command. Follow the instructions that come after it.

2. This will create a package.json file which will have all the information of the project and related packages. This is very useful for version and package controlling. Here is how the Node.js command prompt will look after firing the npm init command:

```
varun@varun-Inspiron-5523: /media/varun/4E286FE2286FC813/Packt/code/chap2/server     ×   varun@varun-Inspiron-5523: ~/workspace/test
        at Function.Module.runMain (module.js:497:10)
        at startup (node.js:119:16)
        at node.js:902:3
varun@varun-Inspiron-5523:/media/varun/4E286FE2286FC813/Packt/code/chap2/server$ npm init
This utility will walk you through creating a package.json file.
It only covers the most common items, and tries to guess sane defaults.

See 'npm help json' for definitive documentation on these fields
and exactly what they do.

Use 'npm install <pkg> --save' afterwards to install a package and
save it as a dependency in the package.json file.

Press ^C at any time to quit.
name: (server) MyWebSocketServer
version: (0.0.0) 0.0.1
description: My First WebSocketServer
entry point: (index.js) server.js
test command:
git repository:
keywords:
author: Varun
license: (BSD-2-Clause)
About to write to /media/varun/4E286FE2286FC813/Packt/code/chap2/server/package.json:

{
  "name": "MyWebSocketServer",
  "version": "0.0.1",
  "description": "My First WebSocketServer",
  "main": "server.js",
  "scripts": {
    "test": "echo \"Error: no test specified\" && exit 1"
  },
  "author": "Varun",
  "license": "BSD-2-Clause"
}

Is this ok? (yes) yes
```

3. Once done, we need to set up the WebSockets package using the `npm install ws` command. This command will install the necessary libraries for the WebSocket connection, which will look like the following:

```
varun@varun-Inspiron-5523: /media/varun/4E286FE2286FC813/Packt/code/chap2/server    ×    varun@varun-Inspiron-5523: ~/workspace/test

varun@varun-Inspiron-5523:/media/varun/4E286FE2286FC813/Packt/code/chap2/server$ ls
package.json
varun@varun-Inspiron-5523:/media/varun/4E286FE2286FC813/Packt/code/chap2/server$ npm install ws
npm WARN package.json MyWebSocketServer@0.0.1 No repository field.
npm WARN package.json MyWebSocketServer@0.0.1 No README data
npm http GET https://registry.npmjs.org/ws
npm http 200 https://registry.npmjs.org/ws
npm http GET https://registry.npmjs.org/ws/-/ws-0.6.3.tgz
npm http 200 https://registry.npmjs.org/ws/-/ws-0.6.3.tgz
npm http GET https://registry.npmjs.org/ultron
npm http GET https://registry.npmjs.org/options
npm http GET https://registry.npmjs.org/nan
npm http 304 https://registry.npmjs.org/options
npm http 200 https://registry.npmjs.org/ultron
npm http GET https://registry.npmjs.org/ultron/-/ultron-1.0.1.tgz
npm http 200 https://registry.npmjs.org/nan
npm http GET https://registry.npmjs.org/nan/-/nan-1.4.1.tgz
npm http 200 https://registry.npmjs.org/ultron/-/ultron-1.0.1.tgz
npm http 200 https://registry.npmjs.org/nan/-/nan-1.4.1.tgz

> ws@0.6.3 install /media/varun/4E286FE2286FC813/Packt/code/chap2/server/node_modules/ws
> (node-gyp rebuild 2> builderror.log) || (exit 0)

ws@0.6.3 node_modules/ws
├── ultron@1.0.1
├── options@0.0.6
└── nan@1.4.1
varun@varun-Inspiron-5523:/media/varun/4E286FE2286FC813/Packt/code/chap2/server$ ls
node_modules  package.json
varun@varun-Inspiron-5523:/media/varun/4E286FE2286FC813/Packt/code/chap2/server$ ls
node_modules  package.json  server.js
varun@varun-Inspiron-5523:/media/varun/4E286FE2286FC813/Packt/code/chap2/server$ nodejs server.js

events.js:72
        throw er; // Unhandled 'error' event
        ^
Error: listen EADDRINUSE
    at errnoException (net.js:901:11)
    at Server._listen2 (net.js:1039:14)
```

 It is possible that you may get some error related to Python. Please ignore it. This library has some other features which require Python to be installed, but the features we are utilizing are not related to Python, so we can ignore it. This error will not affect our development process and our code will work fine.

Now we are ready to code. First, we will create our server JavaScript file named `server.js`, which will be our main server file. Please note that it should be created within the same folder wherein we have run the previous command `npm init`. The server code will look like this:

```
var WebSocketServer = require('ws').Server
wss = new WebSocketServer({ port: 8080 });
wss.on('connection', function connection(ws) {
```

```
ws.on('message', function incoming(message) {
console.log('received: %s', message);
ws.send(message);
});
ws.send('Connected');
});
```

This is a very simple server. Let's go through the code step by step:

1. Here we are just creating an instance of WebSocketServer and defining on which port it should listen. Sometimes port 8080 is not available so you may get an error. Don't worry; you can simply change it by doing the following:

   ```
   var WebSocketServer = require('ws').Server
   wss = new WebSocketServer({ port: 8080 });
   ```

2. Once we have the instance we have to add the connection listener, which is triggered if the connection is established:

   ```
   wss.on('connection', function connection(ws)
   ```

3. Once the connection is established, we need to add the listener for that particular WebSockets connection instance. This instance can be used for many purposes like sending messages:

   ```
   ws.on('message', function incoming(message)
   ```

4. Then comes the message sending part. As we are creating an Echo server, we just need to send the message we received back. So we are using the same message and sending it through the WebSockets instance:

   ```
   ws.send(message);
   ```

5. Once we write the code it is time to test it. We need to start our Node.js server which we can do using the following command:

   ```
   > node server.js
   ```

6. Once the server is started, we just have to change a single line from the client side code, which we developed earlier in the chapter — the server URI that we were hitting. Earlier, we were hitting the www.websocket.org website, but now we have to hit the server we have made. We just replace the URI from ws://demo.websocket.org to ws://localhost:8080 and we are good to go. We can run our client application file the same way we did in our last client application and see the result:

   ```
   var wsUri = "ws://localhost:8080";
   ```

The result will be same as the previous one.

Congratulations! You have just made your first WebSockets Echo application.

Summary

In this chapter, we have learned how to write client and server side code. We understood how Node.js can be used as a server for WebSockets and how we can leverage it to create a small server so quickly.

In the next chapter, we will be making a simple application where we will see how WebSockets can be used.

3
Configuring the Server and Transferring Real-time Data

Data is the heart of any application. And data transfer between the client and server is a very important part of it. We have seen in the last chapter how we can transfer data using WebSockets. Now, we will see how we can utilize it and make an application in which real-time data transfer can be used. Real-time data transfer is mainly used when we have a collaborative application or any application which needs reflection as soon as some of the data changes.

In this chapter, we will cover the following topics:

- Real-time data transfer
- Real-time applications
- Collaborative presentation applications
- Adding collaboration
- Do it yourself
- Tips and tricks

Full-duplex real-time data transfer

As we all know, sending and receiving data as soon as some change happens is real-time data transfer. It can be for some changes that occur in that data. The reason for data change could be user itself or some timed event. In normal scenarios, the user changes should accordingly reflect to other users; for example, chatting applications where people send messages to each other. A chatting application is a very small example of real-time data transfer; let's talk about some big examples like games. Games are the major applications where real-time data transfer is required. But as the industry is growing, our daily use applications are also adopting real-time full-duplex data communication. If we see any stock market application, then we can see live data changes happening, which basically is a good example of server push. In this scenario, the server is pushing data, which is a great feature of WebSockets.

Foundation of real-time applications

We've understood what real-time data transfer is; now let's see what we need to make a real-time data transfer application There are some foundation steps we need to consider before starting any application. Some of the major steps are:

- Selecting the functionality we need to make collaborative or real-time data transfer application
- Selecting the server-side technology to make it possible
- Selecting the client-side technology that integrates easily with the server

These three steps are the main points to keep in mind. As we know, HTML5 supports WebSockets and is one of the best ways of data comunication. Now for the server-side, we have seen how easily and seamlessly the Node.js server can be integrated. Now the most important part is which functionality we need to make real-time. This is based on the kind of application we are building. Next, keeping these points in mind, we will start building our application so that we understand it better.

Collaborative presentation application

Keeping the foundation elements in mind, let's build a presentation application where if you change the presentation, then it will also change for other users and vice versa. Basically, we will build a web-based collaborative presentation sharing application. To make this application for modern browsers, we need a JavaScript library, which gives us all the features we need for a presentation application, such as creating different pages, navigation, and so on. And then we will add the feature that enables collaboration between different users.

The presentation library

There are different JavaScript libraries available from which we can choose. The library that gives us enough features to create our application is **reveal.js**. It is a well-made API and is fully based on HTML5. There is also a well-made application to make online presentations, which is also based on the same JavaScript library that we are going to use. The website for the same is www.slides.com. Go ahead and visit this website; it will give you a feeling of how our presentation is going to look. We will be using this API and making it collaborative so that other users can also change the slide and the reflection can be seen by everyone.

Setting up the library

Firstly, we need to download and set up the library file. The library that we are going to use can be found at https://github.com/hakimel/reveal.js. The following are the steps to set up a library:

1. Download a copy for yourself and open the index.html file.

2. Once you open the file, you can see the default presentation that comes with it.

3. The library reveal.js is a complete presentation solution which comes with its own navigation and presentation mechanism.

4. Here you can use keyboard controls to navigate to different pages. Use the right arrow key to go to the next slide and the left arrow key for the previous slide. Similarly use the up and down arrow keys for different levels of presentation. It supports all kind of text and you can put real code or any HTML content in it which is live. You can go through the slides to know more about the library features.

Adding collaboration

To add the collaborative feature to the presentation library, let's first see what steps we need to follow to make this application work. It is good practice to write down the important steps from the client side and server side just to make sure that we are covering each and every step.

For this application, let's make the list of things to do for the client side:

- Connecting to the WebSocket server
- Receiving messages from WebSocket

- Applying the slide number received from the server to the current presentation
- Sending slide details to the server when the user changes the slide

Now that we have listed the points for the client, let's list down the points for server as well:

- Initializing WebSocket server
- Receiving slides data from client
- Storing current slide data
- Passing current slide data for new users who joined later
- Broadcasting the slide data changes to all the users
- Checking for the slide data changes to reduce duplicate calls

As we have the library downloaded, we need to add our custom client and server-side code to make it work.

Code implementation

The library has most of the code ready for us, so we don't need to add much code for the client. We need to write the server code completely. Let's check out the code.

The client code

On the client side, the main file is index.html, so we are going to add our code to that file. At the end of the JavaScript code in the file, add the following code:

```
function isJson(str)
{
    try
    {
        JSON.parse(str);
    }
    catch (e)
    {
        return false;
    }
    return true;
}

var ws;

var isChangedByMe = true;
```

```
function init()
{
  ws = new WebSocket('ws://localhost:9001');
  //Connection open event handler
    ws.onopen = function(evt)
    {
      ws.send('connection open');
    }
  //Event Handler to receive messages from server
  ws.onmessage = function(message)
  {
      console.log('received: '+ message);
      if(isJson(message.data))
      {
        var obj = JSON.parse(message.data);
        console.log("changing slide to "+ obj.indexh);
        isChangedByMe = false;
        Reveal.slide( obj.indexh, obj.indexv);
      }
  }
  //Adding event handler when slide is changed by use
  Reveal.addEventListener( 'slidechanged', function( event )
  {
      if(isChangedByMe)
      {
        ws.send(JSON.stringify({ 'indexh' :event.indexh , 'indexv'
: event.indexv}));
        console.log("sending slide data : " + event.indexh);
      }
      isChangedByMe = true;
  });
}
//Event handler for application load event
window.addEventListener("load", init, false);
```

Code explanation

Let's see what we have written in this code.

We have added the load event listener to the window so that as soon as we know that the browser window is loaded properly, we can start initializing our WebSocket connection:

```
window.addEventListener("load", init, false);
```

Once the `init` method is called, we write the actual code which communicates with the WebSocket server. Here, in this piece of code, we have instantiated the WebSocket object and written an event handler which will be called when the connection is open. Once the connection is established, this method is invoked and we come to know that the connection has been created. Now we send some random data, which can be treated as the acknowledgment for the server:

```
ws = new WebSocket('ws://localhost:9001');
ws.onopen = function(evt)
 {
    ws.send('connection open');
 }
```

Now, we add the message event handler, which is invoked when the server sends a message — in our case, we have to handle the data that server is going to send us:

```
ws.onmessage = function(message)
```

So you can see that we are calling the `isJson` method and sending the message data to it. This method is invoked to check whether the data we have received is in the format we want or not; otherwise it can throw an error:

```
if(isJson(message.data))
```

After checking that we have the right type of the data, we now parse the data into the **JavaScript Object Notation (JSON)** format. The reason we have to parse the JSON method is because we are sending the data in JSON, which is converted to string:

```
var obj = JSON.parse(message.data)
```

Once the data is converted, we get a JSON object in the obj variable. Now comes one of the important methods, which basically is a reveal.js library method used to set the current slide of the presentation:

```
Reveal.slide( obj.indexh, obj.indexv);
```

This way we receive the data and set it in the presentation. Now comes the second part of the code — sending the data to the server.

The reveal.js library gives us an event which we can listen to and get information about the current slide:

```
Reveal.addEventListener( 'slidechanged', function( event )
```

Once we add the listener to the `slidechanged` event, we can use the data which was passed under the event attribute.

Here is how we have created a string from the JSON object and passed it to the server:

```
ws.send(JSON.stringify({ 'indexh' :event.indexh , 'indexv' :
event.indexv}));
```

In the WebSockets client, we use the send method to send the data to the server. Once sent, the server receives it and performs the action as we have defined. Now let's check how the server is set up and how it behaves.

The server code

We have already seen in the last chapter how we can create a Node.js server. In a similar manner, we will create another application using NPM (please refer to *Chapter 2, Getting Started with WebSockets* for instructions for setting up and running the server). Here is the server code that we need to write in the server.js file:

```
var WebSocketServer = require('ws').Server
    wss = new WebSocketServer({ port: 9001 });

//Broadcast method to send message to all the users
wss.broadcast = function broadcast(data,sentBy)
{
  for(var i in this.clients)
  {
    if(this.clients[i] != sentBy)
    {
      this.clients[i].send(data);
    }
  }
};

//Data holder for current side number
var currentSlideData = { 'indexh' :0 , 'indexv' : 0};
//JSON string parser
function isJson(str)
{
    try
    {
        JSON.parse(str);
    }
    catch (e)
    {
        return false;
    }
}
```

```
    return true;
}


//WebSocket connection open handler
wss.on('connection', function connection(ws)
{
//WebSocket message receive handler
    ws.on('message', function incoming(message)
    {
    if(isJson(message))
    {
      var obj = JSON.parse(message);

        if(currentSlideData.indexv != obj.indexv ||
currentSlideData.indexh != obj.indexh )

        {
          currentSlideData.indexv = obj.indexv;
          currentSlideData.indexh = obj.indexh;
//Broadcasting the message to all the users
          wss.broadcast(message,this);
          console.log('broadcasting data');
        }
    }

      console.log('received: %s', message);

  });

  console.log('sending initial Data');
//When user is connected sending the current slide information for
the users who joined later
  ws.send(JSON.stringify(currentSlideData));

});
```

This code is pretty standard and straightforward. Let's break this down and understand what we have put here and why.

Code explanation

Here, one of the main methods you can see is the `broadcast`. We write this method to broadcast the slide change data to all the users connected using WebSockets. We are simply looping through all the clients and send the data using the `send()` method:

```
wss.broadcast = function broadcast(data,sentBy)
{
  for(var i in this.clients)
  {
    if(this.clients[i] != sentBy)
    {
      this.clients[i].send(data);
    }
  }
};
```

After this, we define a variable in which we will be holding the slide data temporarily. This variable is important because whenever we get the slide data, we will store it and pass it when needed. There is a situation when users join the meeting at a later stage; using this data stored in this variable, we can provide them with the current slide number as stored:

```
var currentSlideData = {'indexh' :0 , 'indexv' : 0};
```

Now look at the following piece of code. Here, we are handling the connection event so that we can pass the current slide number data to the user. This event gives us the indication of the new user. While sending data, you will notice that we have used the `JSON.stringify` method. This method is used to make a string from JSON as our object is in the JSON format:

```
wss.on('connection', function connection(ws)
{
  console.log('sending initial Data');

  ws.send(JSON.stringify(currentSlideData));

});
```

Within this code, we can see that we have one parameter passed: the instance of the WebSocket object for that particular user. To receive messages, we need to add a `message` event handler which you can see in the following code. And the parameter is the actual message which is being passed from the client side:

```
ws.on('message', function incoming(message)
```

After getting the message, we check if the object passed is a JSON or not. So for this we have the JSON method defined, which basically checks for the JSON string and returns true/false. After the check we parse the JSON string and check if the value is similar to the last value of slide index data. If not, we store it and broadcast the message to all the clients. The check is necessary to avoid duplicate calls. Following is the code:

```
if(isJson(message))
   {
     var obj = JSON.parse(message);
       if(currentSlideData.indexv != obj.indexv ||
currentSlideData.indexh != obj.indexh )
       {
         currentSlideData.indexv = obj.indexv;
         currentSlideData.indexh = obj.indexh;
         wss.broadcast(message,this);
         console.log('broadcasting data');
       }
   }
```

And that is all—just a simple server code which is very powerful and works fine for our small applications.

Once we run the application, here is how it will look:

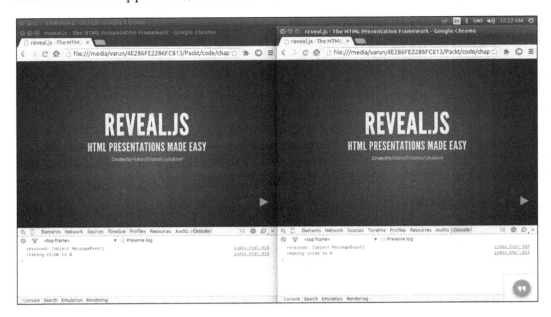

We can see that both have same first slide which is on index zero:

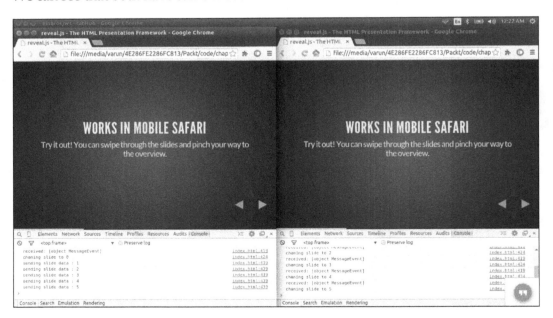

And once we navigate to other slides, the slides for other users also change. Take a look at the **Console** log in the left-hand side window. We can see that **sending slide data** along with slide number is displayed, which shows that upon slide change, the data is being sent. In the right-hand side window, we can see that **changing slide to** is logged in the console, which shows that the data is received from the server and accordingly we see the slide changing for the user.

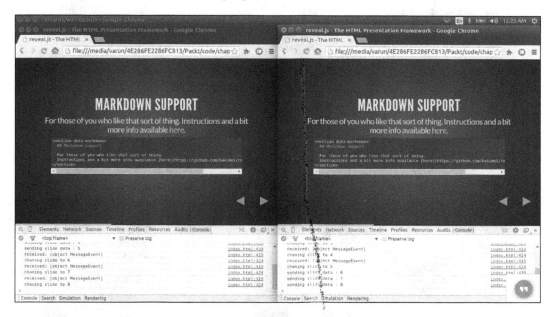

Similarly, if we change the slide from the right-hand side window, it will reflect on the left-hand side window, which is clearly visible from the logs. This same will happen for all users. Following is the screenshot of the logs as seen in the command prompt:

```
●●●   varun@varun-Inspiron-5523: /media/varun/4E286FE2286FC813/Packt/code/chap3/server
received: {"indexh":1,"indexv":0}
broadcasting data
received: {"indexh":0,"indexv":0}
sending initial Data
received: something
sending initial Data
received: something
broadcasting data
received: {"indexh":2,"indexv":0}
broadcasting data
received: {"indexh":1,"indexv":0}
sending initial Data
received: something
sending initial Data
received: something
broadcasting data
received: {"indexh":0,"indexv":0}
broadcasting data
received: {"indexh":1,"indexv":0}
^Cvarun@varun-Inspiron-5523:/media/varun/4E286FE2286FC813/Packt/code/chap3/server$ nodejs server.js
sending initial Data
received: something
sending initial Data
received: something
broadcasting data
received: {"indexh":1,"indexv":0}
broadcasting data
received: {"indexh":2,"indexv":0}
broadcasting data
received: {"indexh":3,"indexv":0}
broadcasting data
received: {"indexh":4,"indexv":0}
broadcasting data
received: {"indexh":5,"indexv":0}
broadcasting data
received: {"indexh":6,"indexv":0}
broadcasting data
received: {"indexh":7,"indexv":0}
broadcasting data
received: {"indexh":8,"indexv":0}
```

On the sever side, we can see the data that is received and the data broadcast logs shows that the data is being passed on to all the users. Putting logs on the server side always helps to check the steps to debug the application.

Do it yourself

This application is a very simple and easy to build application. You have learned how to create a simple application with some limited features. There can be many additions made to this application and it can be made more powerful. Let's give you some tips on features that you can develop.

Input username

Whenever the user visits the URL, the application asks for the username. The username that is inputted is displayed in the top-left corner of the screen. I think this scenario is quite easy to build. I will leave its implementation to you. It is easy up to the point that we want to show the list of users, which is basically our next scenario.

The list of users

Make a button which will show you a list of users that are currently online. This scenario needs code changes both on the client as well the server side. Let me list down some key points that you need to implement this feature:

1. As soon as the user enters the name, save it on the server side. This can be achieved by sending the name of the user in a particular format and handling the same on the server side to store it in the array or object.

2. Maintain a list of all the users on the server side for reference.

3. Fetch the list of users from the server as soon as we join the server. This can be achieved by sending a particular message like `getUsers` and adding another entry on the `message` event handler returning the list of users.

4. Make a button on the UI side and slide in the list of users.

User-based authorization to change the presentation

When the user enters the meeting, ask them whether they want to join as a presenter or attendee. If user chooses to join as a presenter, then allow the user to change the slide. If the user chooses to join as an attendee, then restrict the user from changing the slides.

Asking the user when they enter the name is easy; the slightly complicated part is restricting the user from changing the slides. That is easy if we dig into the configuration of the reveal.js library. In the configuration, we can see some parameters which are true and false. We just need to alter them as per the user type: presenter/attendee.

Making the user the presenter

We have the presenter and the attendee. Now let us make a provision for the presenter to give permission to the attendee. So from the list of users, if the presenter clicks on the user name then it will make that user the presenter.

This can be achieved in a simple way by changing the configuration of reveal.js at runtime. The same configuration that we changed earlier on the basis of role, we just need to invoke the same functionality on the change of role of the user.

Tips and tricks

Let's talk about some tips and tricks that you can use while making an application.

- Using JSON:

  The JSON format is an easily readable format in JavaScript. It is always good to transfer data in the JSON format.

- Object-based structure for WebSockets:

  Normally, in any application where we have to transfer different data sets, it is always preferred that we finalize a proper structure for the messages. Take the example of a chatting application: if we finalize a structure, it is better to handle the message. Here is a sample structure:

  ```
  {
    type: "message"
    data : {
      from: "varun"
      to : "user1"
      data : "hello"
            }
  }
  ```

- Using ArrayBuffer:

  There is another way to send data using ArrayBuffer; you can also send a **Binary Large Object (BLOB)**. Here is an example of the same:

  ```
  var array = new Float32Array(5);
    for(var i = 0; i < array.length; ++i) {
      array[i] = i / 2;
    }
    ws.send(array, { binary: true, mask: true });
  ```

These kinds of structures can help in better understanding and can be used for different sets of messages. Here, the type can be a message, image, audio, file, or anything else. And the property data is generic, which can have the data for all these different types.

Summary

In this chapter, we have seen how HTML5-based JavaScript libraries can be utilized. We have combined WebSockets with the reveal.js library for a collaborative application. This was a simple example, and you have seen that with less coding we have achieved a good working application. You have learned how to configure the server, send and receive data, and broadcast the data from the server to all the clients.

In the coming chapter, we will see the use of another library along with some frameworks, to develop a complete application using modern technologies.

4
Using WebSockets in Real Scenario

We have seen in the last chapter that how to create a real-time presentation sharing application. We understood how real-time data transfer works and how to set up the server. Now we will go to the next step, where we will see what more elements we need to add to strengthen our application in terms of structure with the use of a framework. In this chapter, we will see the different steps to create an application.

The real scenario

The question here is what is a real scenario? We have already seen an application which is a real-world scenario application, but then what we are referring to here? A properly structured application is incomplete without a framework in place. In the last application, we used a JavaScript server and a JavaScript library, did the integration, and built our application. But do you think that the application structure is good enough to support extensibility or reusability? The answer is NO, it is not, because we have not used any framework which will provide better structuring to our application. In this chapter, let's talk about the real scenario where we implement different structures or frameworks for our application.

The JavaScript framework

With the growth of HTML5, JavaScript frameworks are coming into the picture. And the scenario is that we have a lot of them to choose from. Some of the commonly used frameworks are AngularJS, Ember.js, Knockout.js, Backbone.js, and a lot more. We will be using AngularJS in our next example. AngularJS is developed by Google developers and is quite a powerful framework with a lot of needed features.

AngularJS

AngularJS is an open source framework developed by Google. It is based on a very famous design pattern: **Model-View-ViewModel (MVVM)**. Along with that it gives features that work seamlessly with HTML5, such as directives, bindings, and controllers. It mainly handles the problems of single-page applications providing features to implement dynamic views and routing mechanisms to simplify navigation between pages without loading the complete webpage. This feature makes this framework very beneficial for developers. It not only solves the problems of development, but also has made testing very easy.

There are a lot of details available on the Web about the AngularJS framework.

Learn by doing

Learn by doing is one of the best way of learning. Sometimes you learn about something and then implement it. But because you have already read the scenarios, you can implement it easily. One of the best methods is to start doing, and when you face a problem try to find a solution. This will improve your problem-solving skills and will help you explore more. On similar lines, let's start with an application and we will see where we encounter problems and where can we see the need for a framework.

The collaborative drawing application

Let's build a drawing application in which the user can draw on a canvas and other users can also do the same at the same time. Basically, we are creating a collaborative drawing application. Before building the application, let's gather the requirements and do some analysis, which is necessarily required to build an application.

Requirements

Here, our main requirement is that we need to make an application which provides collaborative drawing. So what we need is a client application which is connected to a server and which delivers the data from one user to another in real time. Along with that, we need to make a mechanism using HTML to draw. Instead of spending a lot of time on coding for a drawing feature, we can use a good readymade library that provides us with the features we need for drawing.

So if we make a list of the items needed to build the application, it will look like this:

- Client application
- Server
- Drawing library
- Implementation of real-time data transfer

Now we know what to create. The next step is to divide the tasks for the application.

The drawing library

We chose to go for a library instead of coding the whole thing. There are a few libraries available, but one of best is the **Fabric.js** library. You can download the library from `http://fabricjs.com/`. You can even build a custom library file with selected features to make it lightweight. There are many features that this library provides, all of which you can see on the aforementioned website. Let us see a demo code for the Fabric.js library:

```html
<!DOCTYPE html>
<html>
<head>
</head>
<body>
    <canvas id="canvas" width="300" height="300">
....</canvas>

    <script src="lib/fabric.js">
....</script>

    <script>
        var canvas = new fabric.Canvas('canvas');
        var rect = new fabric.Rect({
            top : 100,
            left : 100,
            width : 60,
            height : 70,
            fill : 'red'
        });
        canvas.add(rect);
    </script>
</body>
</html>
```

We can see in this code how simple this library is. You just need to add the canvas tag and start adding the objects to it, and it will display in the application. This library is quite easy to implement which will help us a lot because we are already dealing with a lot of different things here. Try the code to see what you get in the output and play around the library to get used to it.

The client application

The first step is to make a client application. Here is the code for the client:

```html
<!DOCTYPE html>

<html>

<head>

</head>

<body>

<button id="addCircle">Add Circle</button>

<button id="addRectangle">Add Rectangle</button>

<button id="addTriangle">Add Triangle</button>

<button id="pencil" toggle>Pencil</button>

<button id="selection" toggle>Selection</button>

    <canvas id="canvas" width="1024" height="768"></canvas>

    <script src="lib/fabric.js"></script>

    <script>

//creating canvas instance
        var canvas = new fabric.Canvas('canvas');

//setting some properties for canvas

        canvas.freeDrawingBrush.color = 'green';

        canvas.freeDrawingBrush.lineWidth = 10;
```

```
        canvas.selectable = false;

        canvas.on('path:created',function(e){

            console.log(JSON.stringify(e));

        })

//main initialize method
        function init()

        {

            pencil.addEventListener('click', pencilHandler);

            addCircle.addEventListener('click', addCircleHandler);

            addRectangle.addEventListener('click',
addRectangleHandler);

            addTriangle.addEventListener('click',
addTriangleHandler);

            selection.addEventListener('click', function(){

                canvas.isDrawingMode = false;

            })

        }

//changing the drawing mode to free drawing
        function pencilHandler()

        {

            canvas.isDrawingMode = true;

        }

//adding circle to the canvas
        function addCircleHandler()
```

```
            {
                var circle = new fabric.Circle({

                    radius: 20,

                    fill: 'green',

                    left: 100,

                    top: 100

                });

                canvas.add(circle);

            }

    //adding rectangle to the canvas
            function addRectangleHandler()

            {

                var rect = new fabric.Rect({

                    top : 100,

                    left : 100,

                    width : 60,

                    height : 70,

                    fill : 'red'

                });

                canvas.add(rect);

            }

    //adding triangle to the canvas
            function addTriangleHandler()
```

```
    {

        var triangle = new fabric.Triangle({

            width: 20,

            height: 30,

            fill: 'blue',

            left: 50,

            top: 50

        });

        canvas.add(triangle);

    }

//adding window load event
        window.addEventListener("load", init, false);

    </script>

</body>

</html>
```

In this code, we have created a canvas and made some buttons to add different shapes onto the canvas. One important feature added is that of free drawing. Copy and paste the code into the index.html file and try running it. If you read the Fabric.js library, you will come to know how it works. Don't forget to download the library file and include the library in the code.

Integrating with the server

As we have done the coding for the basic client feature, we now have to integrate the application with the server using WebSockets. For that, we need to first find out what data we need to send to the server. For collaboration, we have to send data about the shapes we need to create on the other user's canvas. Let's list the set of actions we need to carry out on the client and server side.

Client:

- Capture the event for the add shape button
- Send the object to the server
- Create a WebSocket connection to the server
- Capture server data
- Handle and add the objects received from the server to the canvas

Server:

- Create a WebSocket server
- Receive the data
- Pass the data to all the connected clients

On the basis of the preceding list of items, we have made some changes to the code from both the server and the client side.

The client code

We will now implement the code as per the listed items for server communication in our client-side code, which will have code to communicate with the server. Following is the client code which has been changed according to the client items:

```
<!DOCTYPE html>
<html>
  <head>
  </head>
  <body>
    <button id="addCircle">Add Circle</button>
    <button id="addRectangle">Add Rectangle</button>
    <button id="addTriangle">Add Triangle</button>
    <button id="pencil" toggle>Pencil</button>
    <button id="selection" toggle>Selection</button>
    <canvas id="canvas" width="1024" height="768"></canvas>
    <script src="lib/fabric.js"></script>
    <script>
      //creating canvas instance
            var canvas = new fabric.Canvas('canvas');

      //setting some properties for canvas
            canvas.freeDrawingBrush.color = 'green';
```

```
canvas.freeDrawingBrush.lineWidth = 10;

canvas.selectable = false;

canvas.on('path:created',function(e){

    console.log(JSON.stringify(e));

})
```

```
//main initialize method
    function init()

    {

        initServer();

        pencil.addEventListener('click', pencilHandler);

        addCircle.addEventListener('click',
addCircleHandler);

        addRectangle.addEventListener('click',
    addRectangleHandler);

        addTriangle.addEventListener('click',
    addTriangleHandler);

        selection.addEventListener('click', function(){

            canvas.isDrawingMode = false;

        })

    }
```

```
//changing the drawing mode to free drawing
    function pencilHandler()

    {

        canvas.isDrawingMode = true;

    }
```

```
//add circle to the canvas
    function addCircleHandler()

        {

            var obj = {

                radius: 20,

                fill: 'green',

                left: 100,

                top: 100

            };

            // var circle = new fabric.Circle(obj);

            // canvas.add(circle);
//sending the circle object to the server
            sendObject('Circle',obj);

        }

    //add rectangle to the canvas
        function addRectangleHandler()

        {

            var obj = {

                top : 100,

                left : 100,

                width : 60,

                height : 70,

                fill : 'red'

            };
```

```
            var rect = new fabric.Rect(obj);

            // canvas.add(rect);
//sending the rectangle object to the server
            sendObject('Rectangle',obj);


        }


//add triangle to the canvas
 function addTriangleHandler()

        {

            var obj = {

                width: 20,

                height: 30,

                fill: 'blue',

                left: 50,

                top: 50

            };

            var triangle = new fabric.Triangle(obj);

            // canvas.add(triangle);
//sending the object to server
            sendObject('Rectangle',obj);


        }

//generic method to add object to the canvas
        function addObject(type,obj)

        {

            var shape;
```

```
if(type == 'Triangle')

{

    shape = new fabric.Triangle(obj);

}

else if(type == 'Rectangle')

{

    shape = new fabric.Rect(obj);

}

 else if(type == 'Circle')

{

    shape = new fabric.Circle(obj);

}

canvas.add(shape);

}

//check for JSON string
function isJson(str)

{

try

{

    JSON.parse(str);

}

catch (e)

{
```

```
                    return false;

            }

            return true;

    }

    var ws;

//method to send object to the server
    function sendObject(type,obj)

    {

        ws.send(JSON.stringify({'type': type,'data' : obj}));

    }

    function connectionOpen()

    {

         ws.send('connection open');

    }
//method handler when message is received from server
    function onMessageFromServer(message)

    {

        console.log('received: '+ message);

        if(isJson(message.data))

        {

            var obj = JSON.parse(message.data)

            console.log("got data from server");

            addObject(obj.type,obj.data)

        }
```

```
        }

//initialize server method
        function initServer()

        {

                ws = new WebSocket('ws://localhost:9001');

                ws.onopen = connectionOpen;


                ws.onmessage = onMessageFromServer;

        }

        window.addEventListener("load", init, false);


    </script>
  </body>
</html>
```

Code explanation

We have already seen in the previous chapter how to send and receive data from the WebSocket server. One of the methods we coded here to send the data is sendObject, which sends the type and the properties of the object to the server:

```
function sendObject(type,obj)

    {
        ws.send(JSON.stringify({'type': type,'data' : obj}));
    }
```

Here one of the main methods is addObject. Once we get the data from the server, we get two properties: one is type and other is the object which has the property's values. These are the values we send to the server and then check the type of the object and add it to the canvas using respective methods:

```
function addObject(type,obj)

    {

        var shape;
```

```
if(type == 'Triangle')

{

    shape = new fabric.Triangle(obj);

}

else if(type == 'Rectangle')

{

    shape = new fabric.Rect(obj);

}

 else if(type == 'Circle')

{

    shape = new fabric.Circle(obj);

}

canvas.add(shape);

}
```

The rest of the code is pretty simple and straightforward.

The server code

Let's now see what needs to be done on the server side. The following code will show what we need to write on the server side:

```
var WebSocketServer = require('ws').Server
    wss = new WebSocketServer({

        port: 9001

    });

//method to broadcast message to all the users
wss.broadcast = function broadcast(data, sentBy)
```

```
{

    for (var i in this.clients)

    {

        this.clients[i].send(data);

    }

};

function isJson(str)

{

    try

    {

        JSON.parse(str);

    }

    catch (e)

    {

        return false;

    }

    return true;

}

//client connection open method
wss.on('connection', function connection(ws)

{
//client message receive method
    ws.on('message', function incoming(message)

    {
```

```
        if (isJson(message))

        {
//broadcasting message to all users
            wss.broadcast(message, this);

            console.log('broadcasting data');

        }

        console.log('received: %s', message);

    });

    console.log('sending initial Data');

});
```

Code explanation

On the server side, we have not done much coding. It is almost the same as the last chapter's server code. We received the data and broadcast it to all connected users.

Do it yourself

This application is a very simple and easy-to-build application. We have seen how to create a simple application with some limited features. Many additions can be added to this application to make it more powerful. Let's give you some tips and information on features that you can develop.

User registration

Whenever the user opens the URL, a log-in/sign-up dialog box will open. User details such as his/her name will be displayed in the top-left corner of the screen.

 This scenario will need a database connection. There are some databases available which can be easily connected to our Node.js server, such as **MongoDB**. I will leave its method of implementation to you. For help in connecting Node.js and MongoDB, visit http://mongodb.github.io/node-mongodb-native/.

The list of users

Make a button which will show you a list of users that are currently online. This scenario needs code changes both on the client as well as the server side. Let me list down some key points that you need to implement this feature:

- We are already saving the list of users in the database once you have developed the user registration functionality. We can maintain a list of all online users or we can just keep the list on the server. The problem with persisting the data on the server is that it will be erased once the server restarts.

- Fetch the list of users from the server as soon as we join the server. This can be achieved by sending a particular message, such as getOnlineUsers, and adding another entry to the message event handler returning the list of users.

- Display the list of users on the screen so that you can see a proper online users list. This needs changes on the client side.

Share with specific users

As we have already implemented a list of users, we can now implement user-based drawing sharing. In this, we can share our drawings with some specific users only.

 This can be achieved by adding another parameter to the object we are sending to the server to add the object: the target user ID. This user id is unique for users and used to identify a user. This will help us in identifying and send the data to a specific user only.

Save drawings

Once we are done with the drawing, we can save it and make it available for future use.

 We have to connect our application to a database which can hold the values that we have already achieved in earlier scenario. Now we need to add another table in the database just to store the drawing. Fabric.js gives us an object of all the drawing elements that we have drawn, and we can make a JSON string and store it in the database for future use.

The application structure

Structuring the application is a really important part. If we look at the code we have written, we can see that it does not have a good structure. The structure has to be such that in the future if we want add some features to it, it should be easy to do so. And code should be written in such a way that it is easily maintainable. To achieve this, we need to use some sort of a structure, which is called a framework. Frameworks are designed to give a sense of structure to the application.

Restructure the application

Now that we know about frameworks, let's restructure our application using the AngularJS framework. Let's see what we can restructure here; we will divide everything into model, view, controller, and service layers. Let's see what these terms are and where they fit in our application.

Model

In our application, we have not seen the need to store data, but if we want to extend our application and add more features, then there will be a need for a **Model**. As we have seen in some scenarios where we have a list of users and drawings, we need the Model to store the data on the client side so that it is easily accessible for use. AngularJS provides good features to store the data and the binding helps in showing the list data very easily in the UI.

View

An application is normally divided into different views, but in our application we just have one view. As we have seen in the scenarios, we need a login screen for users. In that scenario, we need a different view to be set up, and here Views come into the picture. AngularJS provides us a very easy way to maintain our Views. The routing mechanism of AngularJS also helps us in navigating between different views providing browser history as well as maintaining a single-page application.

Controller

As the application is divided into different views, we also need different controllers which basically control the UI behavior and help in communicating with the services. AngularJS controllers are very powerful and implement **Dependency Injection** (**DI**), which helps in injecting services, models, and so on to the controller to be operated in the View.

Service

Service is very important when we have an application that connects to a server. Maintaining one place for server communication is a good approach as it creates different layers in the application, which can be manipulated without affecting the other layers of the application.

As we read and understand about the different patterns of structuring application using the AngularJS framework, I would highly recommend that you start implementing the same application using AngularJS. It is an excellent framework which fulfills all the needs of a developer and it is a fully loaded framework.

Summary

In this chapter, we have seen how HTML5-based JavaScript libraries can be utilized. We have combined WebSockets with the Fabric.js library for a collaborative application. We have also seen how an application can be divided into parts and created. We have seen the development flow and learned about the structuring of the application as well.

In the next chapter, we will see the behavior of WebSocket and its implementation on mobile and tablets.

5
WebSockets for Mobile and Tablet

WebSockets work great on the Web and have a good performance. We have seen how easy and powerful WebSockets are to implement on the web. With the growth of mobile phones, the need for applications to shift from desktop to mobile has become very important. In this chapter, we will focus on how WebSocket behaves and its implementation on mobile and tablets.

Mobile devices and the WebSocket

The whole world is moving to mobile devices; then why shouldn't we? Mobiles have become very powerful and they can do what a computer can do. Similarly, browsers have become very powerful and they have also started adopting HTML5. Not only browsers, even application support has increased. Lots of applications are available with lots of features. And here, WebSockets plays an important role: whenever there is a need for real-time data transfer, WebSockets are there to help us out. Let's see a few instances where WebSockets can be helpful:

- Chatting applications
- Video conferencing
- Gaming
- Dashboard with real-time data update
- Stock application
- Sports score applications
- Real-time data updates

Now all these applications can be made on the Web and the same is compatible with browsers, thanks to modern browsers that support HTML5.

To implement WebSockets on mobile, there are some libraries available that can be used. The need is to provide a consistent way of implementing WebSockets in different backend technologies. There are some libraries which provide these:

- Pusher
- Socket.IO

Pusher

Pusher is a famous library which helps you to make real-time applications. You can find it at `http://www.pusher.com`. It is a set of libraries built to be integrated with different applications which are built on different servers, such as Ruby on Rails, Python, PHP, and Node. Not only on the server side, they also provide support for JavaScript-based applications along with iOS and Android devices as well.

Pusher is an event-based API and implements a publisher/subscriber mechanism. Here, subscriber is the server and publisher is the client. Subscriber subscribes to the events and publisher triggers those events which the subscriber listens to. To achieve this functionality, publisher and subscriber implement WebSockets internally, which basically provides a real-time experience.

Another big advantage of the Pusher API is that it has a fallback mechanism where when WebSockets is not available, for instance, in some older browser versions, then it uses other technologies such as Flash internally to send the data across. This gives an upper hand to this library so that we don't need to have a different implementation for different browsers and devices.

Socket.IO

Socket.IO is another library completely based on JavaScript. Not only the client side, it completely supports the Node.js server as well. This library provides high performance real-time data transfer and it uses WebSockets under the hood. You can make all kinds of real-time collaborative applications using this API.

Running server on mobile

Till now we were working on a local server and application, but to run the application on a mobile, we need to shift our client application code to a server in such a way that it will cater to the application from a server URL. For this we will take a simple example: basically, we are going to change an application we have already created. In *Chapter 2, Getting Started with WebSockets*, we developed an application for Echo test, which basically returns whatever we send to the server. Now let's see how it will work on a mobile phone.

Firstly, we will change the server code so that it caters to the client code. Here are the changes we will make on the server side:

```
var express = require('express');

var app = express()

var http = require('http').Server(app);

app.use(express.static(__dirname + '/public'));

app.get('/', function(req, res)
{

  res.sendfile('public/index.html');

});

http.listen(3000, function()
{

  console.log('listening on *:3000');

});

var WebSocketServer = require('ws').Server
  , wss = new WebSocketServer({ port: 9001 });

wss.on('connection', function connection(ws)
{

  ws.on('message', function incoming(message)
  {
```

```
        console.log('received: %s', message);

    ws.send(message);

  });

  ws.send('Connected');

});
```

Here we have not done anything specific to the mobile; we have just created another server which provides us with the main client files. We have used an `Express.js` server here, which is helpful in delivering the content through the server. You can read more about an Express.js server and how it works on the Internet. Here, our main focus is just to create a server that will listen on a particular port. So when anyone hits that particular URL, we will get the client application running on the browser.

To install Express.js server, we just need to run the following command:

npm install express

This package needs to be installed in the same directory as of the our `server.js` file. This is important because our server will run and use this package and if not found then server may not work the way we want and throw an error.

Here, we are listening on the `3000` port, so whenever we open `http://localhost:3000`, it will open the specified file. We have defined the file under the `public` folder, `index.html`. So, the first file that will be opened for us is the `index.html` file and we will see its contents. Just like we have done in the earlier chapters, we are doing the same coding for the client side code as well and there is literally no change in it. Only the location of the file has changed and nothing else.

 Make sure that the all the client code and its related libraries will go in the `public` folder because we are picking it from public folder, if not properly placed error may occur.

Once the changes are made you can start the server and check it in the browser to see whether it is working or not. As you listen on the `3000` port, just run `http://localhost:3000` in your browser and make sure the application is running fine.

Local server on mobile

Once the changes are done, we need to run the local server on our mobile phone. This seems difficult but actually it is not. Google Chrome provides us with a great feature through which we can use our local server on mobile browsers as well. Here are the steps we need to implement to run a local server on mobile:

1. Start USB debugging in your mobile/tablet device.
2. Connect your device using USB to your computer.
3. Open the Chrome browser and go to `chrome:/inspect`.
4. This will inspect the connected devices.
5. Now the main setting we need to consider is **Port forwarding**. We are using two different ports: `3000` for the client and `9001` for the WebSocket server. Just make sure you add both of them in the **Port forwarding settings**.

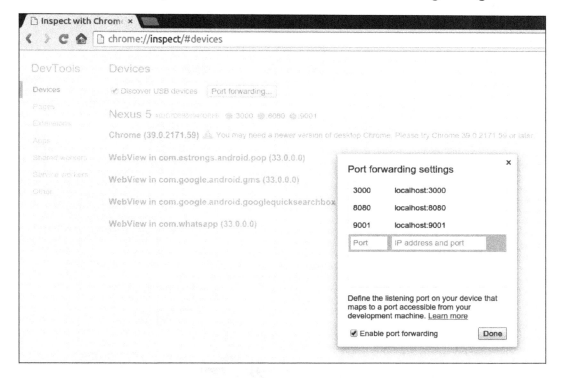

 If you are still facing problems in setting up your mobile device, then visit `https://developer.chrome.com/devtools/docs/remote-debugging`. You will get all the details on how to set up your mobile device.

6. Once these settings are done, you are good to go. Just open the Chrome browser in your mobile device and open the server URL `http://localhost:3000` and see the magic. You will see the same output as we seen on the desktop.

We are able to achieve this output behavior in a very simple fashion just because of HTML5, as HTML5 shows consistent behavior in almost all browsers and it is being adopted by most browsers. This gives us the benefit of making our application using HTML5 WebSockets and having it run almost everywhere. The one thing we need to make sure while building an application is that it has responsive design, as mobile devices have different resolutions and different screen sizes. This is a major problem that needs to be taken care of while creating an application. But thanks to HTML5, we have media queries which give us a feature to handle such scenarios easily.

Mobile output

As you can see, there is no change in the output of the application. It is exactly the same as we have seen on desktop.

Browser support

HTML5 is being adopted by almost all browsers even in mobile and tablet devices. This gives us an upper hand while using a WebSocket application in almost all modern browsers. To check which mobile browsers are supported, visit http://caniuse.com/#feat=websockets, which gives us a list of all the browsers that support WebSockets.

Do it yourself

It's time to do it yourself: creating an application for a mobile device is as easy as it is for the desktop. Now let's transform some of our applications for mobile.

Scenario 1

As we have developed a presentation sharing and drawing application, we will now make them available for mobile as well.

> This is a very easy task: as we know, we just have to change the server so that it provides the client application and we are good. The reason that we don't have to change anything else is that the libraries we have used for the application are so well-written that they can adapt to the mobile view as well. Just try it out.

Here is how it will look when you open the presentation sharing application on mobile:

Scenario 2

The server is going to be the same, but you can play around with the client application interface to make it responsive as per the device screen size, which can be achieved using **Bootstrap**-like libraries. And for real-time data transfer, you can use the Socket.IO API which is really easy to use and implement.

Create a chat application for desktop and mobile

For this, you need to create a server which just takes a message and broadcasts it to all. And the client will be simple so that it just sends a message to the server. It is pretty simple and straightforward, but the catch is that you need to make it for desktop as well as mobile.

Please see the following image for reference:

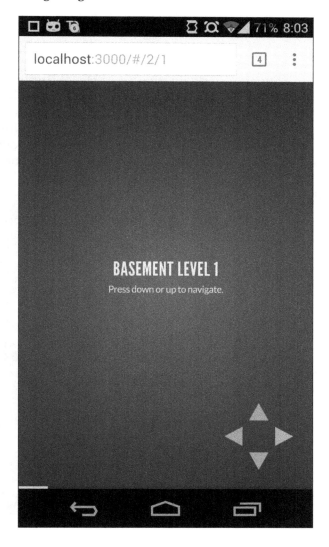

Scenario 3

Make a question game in which you can ask a question, just by entering the question and its options using a user interface. The other person will get the question and answer it. As soon as it is answered, you will receive it right away.

 Just like a chat application, you can use the same Socket.IO API to send the data. The rest is all easy—as soon as user answers the question, you can send it using the API.

Summary

We have seen in this chapter how easy it is to code in HTML5 utilizing its features to provide a device-independent application. WebSockets support is available in almost all modern browsers, and this has made our life easy in terms of developing consistent applications—we don't have to write different code for different devices. We have also seen how Node.js provides flexibility and great support for different devices. In this chapter, we have explored different mobile applications and some APIs which help us in implementing WebSockets, along with how to set up a local server to run applications.

In the next chapter, we will see how to enhance the HTML5 web application development using modern tools.

6
Enhancing HTML5 Web Application Development Using Modern Tools

HTML5 is a modern specification which defines a lot of features that we have seen in the previous chapters. One of the biggest problems faced in application development is code management: how you will structure your application so that it will be easily readable, expandable, maintainable, and so on. In this chapter, we will see modern methods or tools of modern application development. Once we come to know about the different techniques, methods, and tools, we will be equipped to enhance our application.

Modern tools and techniques

There are many different tools and techniques that enable the development process to be seamless. Let's talk about some of the modern tools and techniques that make a developer's life easier:

- Code editors
- Boilerplates
- Packaging tools
- Build tools
- Application frameworks
- Modern servers
- Responsive web design

Code editors

The first thing to choose before we start coding is the editor that we will use for coding. There are many editors available, but the one most preferred is **Sublime Text**. It is a free-to-use tool and has really good support for different technologies.

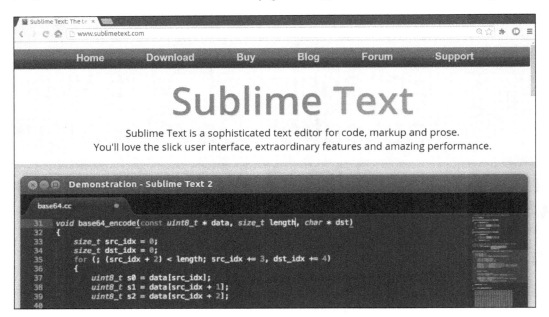

Some of the features that Sublime offers are as follows:

- Navigation to anywhere in the document by just pressing *Ctrl+Shift+P*
- Distraction-free mode
- Great plugin API based on Python that you can experiment with
- Package Control that provides a lot of different packages to choose from and work on any technology you would like to

Boilerplates

These are nothing but different readymade templates which help in accelerating the process. As we all know what templates are and how they will help, let's see some of the examples of boilerplate:

- We can get a boilerplate plugin in Sublime Text, which is very useful during application development.

- There are some boilerplates that help you create the complete code folder structure; one of them is `https://html5boilerplate.com/`.

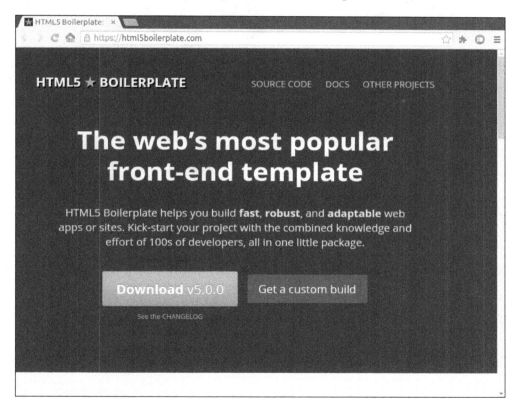

- Yeoman is another tool that helps in starting up a project quickly and can be found at `http://yeoman.io/`. It is a very powerful tool; it not only helps in quickly starting applications but also provides workflow for these applications. It is mainly a tool to make you productive during different phases of the development process. It also provides you with a feature to make your own build configuration.

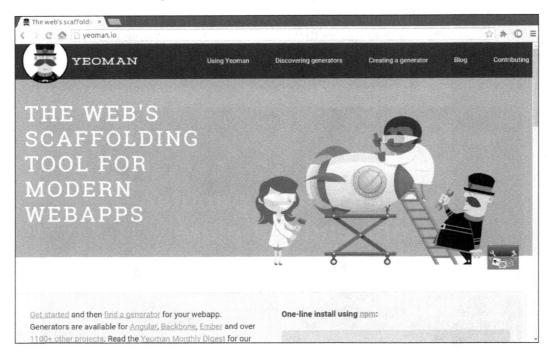

Packaging tools

As the application grows in size, it becomes difficult to manage when there are different dependencies. In an environment when there are several different people working on the same project, we need to take care of the versions and dependencies. This problem is solved by package managers. One of the most popular package managers for modern technologies is NPM. NPM gives you a very simple way to maintain your packages and install them.

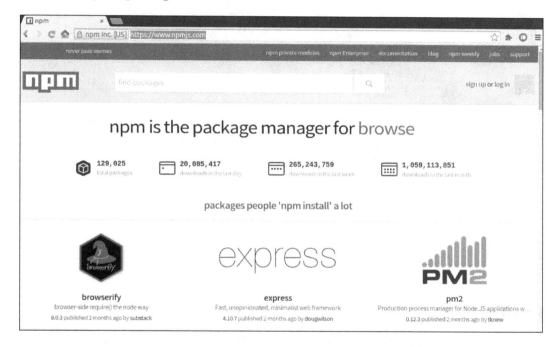

In previous chapters, we used WebSocket and Express.js packages in our application and we installed them with just a single command. The Package Manager made it easy to make packages of different modules of the application and publish them as well. There are a number of different packages available which we can utilize to make our application better.

Bower is also one of the very useful tools that provides package management. It basically manages all things for you, such as finding, downloading, and saving dependencies by itself using one configuration file.

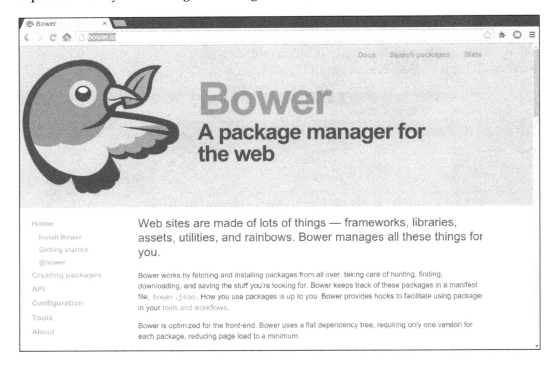

Build tools

When we make an application and the code length increases, we use build tools to build the application to get an optimized, compiled, tested, and automated process. Build tools are really helpful in providing optimized applications to users. Automation is the biggest advantage of build tools; it just does everything on its own for you. Now let's look at some great, simple, and modern build tools for HTML5 and JavaScript-based applications:

- **Grunt**: The JavaScript task runner (http://gruntjs.com/)

- **Brunch**: HTML5 build tool(http://brunch.io/)

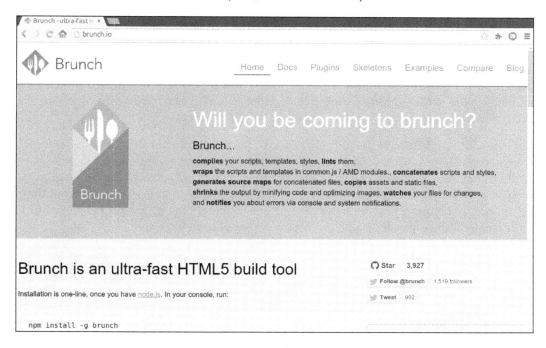

Application frameworks

Giving an application a proper structure is a key thing to implement in the development process. Many applications fail when they grow all because of their structure; if the foundation is bad, then no matter how big the building you make is—it will fall one day. On a similar line, we have to think about structuring our applications as well. There are many different frameworks available that we can use and some of the popular ones are:

- AngularJS
- Ember.js
- Backbone.js
- Ext JS

Modern servers

Servers were always a problem for web developers because though there were options, they used different technologies. It is always an overhead to learn another technology. However, Node.js, which is a JavaScript server, solves this issue. We have already seen how it works. There are a lot of different packages available for the Node.js server also, which you can use to make your application better.

Responsive web design

UI has always been the key element of any application. Earlier, we used to open applications and websites only on computers. But now things are changing; mobiles and tablets are coming into the picture and capturing the market. Now companies are launching web versions of their application or website. Due to this phase, developers have made the same website for mobile devices, too. This is a costly thing to do because it involves all the lifecycle phases of an application.

However, with modern HTML5 technologies, we don't have to think much about it, as this technology is already equipped with the functionality: there are features in HTML5 that can help us make the same website look good or responsive. Responsive means that the website adapts itself as per the screen size. If it is a small screen, then it does not just show a smaller version of the actual website; instead it rescales and readjusts in such a way that all the content is readable to the user.

Again, implementing this needs changes in the website at different places, but we have different libraries already built which help us in making highly responsive websites in very little time. One of the most frequently used libraries is Bootstrap. This library not only gives you the ability to make your website responsive easily, it provides you with a complete set of different UI controls as well.

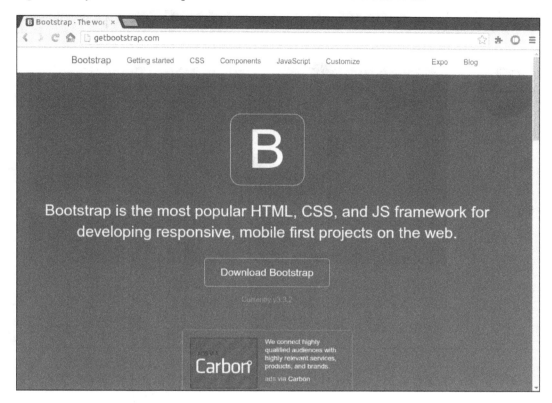

One of the best examples of responsive UI is the website `http://foodsense.is/`. They have really worked on each and every detail of the UI. If you open the website, you won't feel the difference, but when you start to reduce the width of the browser window, you will be able to notice changes. These changes are small and useful: the buttons become smaller but the main content is perfectly fine. And as you keep reducing the width, it keeps changing and gives a perfect readable website even in a small width, which basically shows how the website will look on mobile devices.

Let's see how the UI changes or adapts when we change the size of the browser:

- **In normal state on the desktop**: There you can see that it is just like any other website—a menu bar, an image slider, some buttons, and a subscribe option.

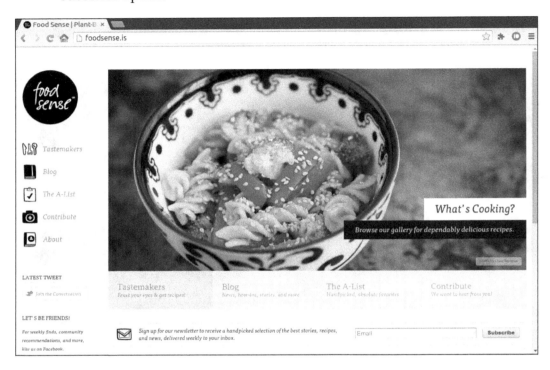

- **In tablet size**: When we reduce the size of the window to that of a tablet, we can notice the changes. The left menu bar is on top now and the details on the button below the image slider are fewer. So the website just shows what is needed and hides some details as the screen size is smaller.

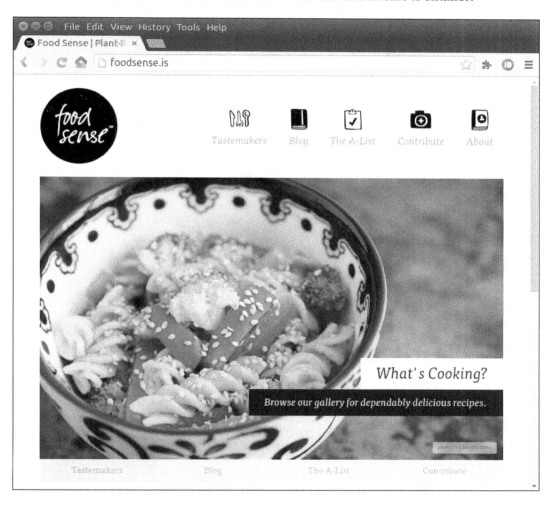

- **In mobile size**: Now when we reduce the window size to the width of a mobile, we can see the menu is on top followed by the logo and the slider. Basically, the items are vertically stacked, which is the best view for mobile devices. We have seen how the UI changes as we change the width; this is all possible due to the media queries feature in HTML5.

The MEAN stack

For complete application development, one of the best tools is the MEAN stack. MEAN stands for:

- M for MongoDB

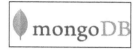

- E for Express.js framework

- A for AngularJS

- N for Node.js

The MEAN stack gives us modern technologies to build web applications. To create any application we need a server, a database, and a client framework. And all these are considered in the MEAN stack and seamlessly integrate with each other, helping developers to build big applications.

There is a library available at `http://mean.io/` which gives you the complete MEAN stack and helps you to manage application development as well. Because of the packaging manager, using these libraries is really easy and helpful in accelerating the development process.

Summary

This book has exposed us to different technologies for fast application development. We have seen enhancements of HTML5; we learned how WebSockets works. We have developed some applications based on HTML5 and WebSockets. WebSockets is one of the best methods of communication which provides some great features, such as full-duplex communication which allows the client as well as the server to push the data. We understood how Node.js-based servers can be very useful and easy to implement along with WebSocket server. We achieved and saw different examples of full-duplex communication using WebSockets. We got some exposure to different JavaScript-based libraries which provide readymade components for us to use. We have also seen WebSockets work on mobile devices and seen and understood the different mobile web design features of HTML5. And finally, we have seen different tools and techniques that can help in accelerating the development process of an application. The techniques not only help, but also give your application a new look and feel. Managing dependencies is made easy using package managers. All these modern tools, the accelerated development offered by the MEAN stack, and responsive web design will enable you to make modern applications which work on all devices.

Index

Thank you for buying
WebSocket Essentials – Building Apps with HTML5 WebSockets

About Packt Publishing

Packt, pronounced 'packed', published its first book, *Mastering phpMyAdmin for Effective MySQL Management*, in April 2004, and subsequently continued to specialize in publishing highly focused books on specific technologies and solutions.

Our books and publications share the experiences of your fellow IT professionals in adapting and customizing today's systems, applications, and frameworks. Our solution-based books give you the knowledge and power to customize the software and technologies you're using to get the job done. Packt books are more specific and less general than the IT books you have seen in the past. Our unique business model allows us to bring you more focused information, giving you more of what you need to know, and less of what you don't.

Packt is a modern yet unique publishing company that focuses on producing quality, cutting-edge books for communities of developers, administrators, and newbies alike. For more information, please visit our website at www.packtpub.com.

About Packt Open Source

In 2010, Packt launched two new brands, Packt Open Source and Packt Enterprise, in order to continue its focus on specialization. This book is part of the Packt Open Source brand, home to books published on software built around open source licenses, and offering information to anybody from advanced developers to budding web designers. The Open Source brand also runs Packt's Open Source Royalty Scheme, by which Packt gives a royalty to each open source project about whose software a book is sold.

Writing for Packt

We welcome all inquiries from people who are interested in authoring. Book proposals should be sent to author@packtpub.com. If your book idea is still at an early stage and you would like to discuss it first before writing a formal book proposal, then please contact us; one of our commissioning editors will get in touch with you.

We're not just looking for published authors; if you have strong technical skills but no writing experience, our experienced editors can help you develop a writing career, or simply get some additional reward for your expertise.

Getting Started with HTML5 WebSocket Programming

ISBN: 978-1-78216-696-2   Paperback: 110 pages

Develop and deploy your first secure and scalable real-time web application

1. Start real-time communication in your web applications.

2. Create a feature-rich WebSocket chat application.

3. Learn the step-by-step configuration of the server and clients.

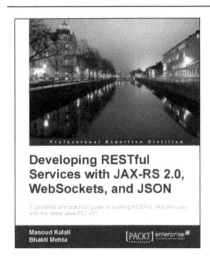

Developing RESTful Services with JAX-RS 2.0, WebSockets, and JSON

ISBN: 978-1-78217-812-5   Paperback: 128 pages

A complete and practical guide to building RESTful web Services with the latest Java EE7 API

1. Learning about different client/server communication models including but not limited to client polling, Server-Sent Events and WebSockets.

2. Efficiently use WebSockets, Server-Sent Events, and JSON in Java EE applications.

3. Learn about JAX-RS 2.0 new features and enhancements.

Please check **www.PacktPub.com** for information on our titles

Socket.IO Real-time Web Application Development

ISBN: 978-1-78216-078-6   Paperback: 140 pages

Build modern real-time web applications powered by Socket.IO

1. Understand the usage of various socket.io features like rooms, namespaces, and sessions.

2. Secure the socket.io communication.

3. Deploy and scale your socket.io and Node.js applications in production.

HTML5 Web Application Development By Example Beginner's guide

ISBN: 978-1-84969-594-7   Paperback: 276 pages

Learn how to build rich, interactive web applications from the ground up using HTML5, CSS3, and jQuery

1. Packed with example applications that show you how to create rich, interactive applications and games.

2. Shows you how to use the most popular and widely supported features of HTML5.

3. Full of tips and tricks for writing more efficient and robust code while avoiding some of the pitfalls inherent to JavaScript.

Please check **www.PacktPub.com** for information on our titles